bodymatters

IS HELEN
pregnant?
Janine amos

CHERRYTREE BOOKS

bodymatters

Kate Smokes Cigarettes
Jon Drinks Alcohol
Why Won't Kim Eat?
Is Helen Pregnant?
Alex Does Drugs
Jamal is Overweight

A Cherrytree Book

First published 2002
by Cherrytree Press
327 High Street
Slough
Berkshire
SL1 1TX

© Evans Brothers Limited 2002

British Library Cataloguing in Publication Data

Amos, Janine
Is Helen Pregnant?. - (Bodymatters)
1. Pregnancy - Juvenile literature
I. Title
618.2

ISBN 1842341073

Printed in Hong Kong by Wing King Tong Co Ltd

Acknowledgements
Planning and production: Discovery Books
Editor: Patience Coster
Photographer: David Simson
Designer: Keith Williams
Artwork: Fred van Deelen
Consultant: Dr Gillian Rice

**All the characters appearing in this book
are played by models.**

Picture acknowledgements
The publisher would like to thank the following
for permission to reproduce their pictures:
Science Photo Library 15 (D Phillips); Chris
Fairclough 23; Photofusion 29 (Paul Baldesare).

LEARNING
SUPPORT
SERVICES

Please return
on or before
the last date
stamped below

0 5 JUN 2014

A FINE WILL BE CHARGED FOR OVERDUE ITEMS

IS HELEN pregnant?

contents

Sophie is there too. They are listening to music in Jo's bedroom.

'It's the school disco next Friday!' says Jo. 'I can wear my new top!' She holds it up against her.

'I hope Tom's going to the disco,' says Helen dreamily. Sophie and Jo roll their eyes. Helen has been talking about Tom, a boy in their class, for weeks.

Sophie flicks through the pages of a magazine. 'There's something here on kissing!' she says. She reads it out to the others: 'Ten Top Tips for Giving the Perfect Kiss!'

Helen sits up. 'Oh, imagine kissing

4

relationships. They often contain popular problem pages, too, where readers' concerns about life and love are discussed.

It can be helpful for teenagers to have their questions answered in magazines. By reading that others have the same worries, it can help you to feel less alone, and that's very important. But the magazines have their downside too. All those pages about boyfriends and girlfriends may make you feel left behind. Sometimes you may feel that everyone has a boyfriend or a girlfriend except you. Don't worry. Whatever the magazines may suggest, most young teenagers are still finding out about the opposite sex as friends.

Teenage magazines

The articles contained in teenage magazines – about music, fashion and celebrities – focus on the interests of most young people. Teenage magazines also have lots of features dealing with boy-girl

boy-girl
relationships

5

Tom Hennessy!' she squeals.
'I think I'd die of excitement!'
Jo and Sophie groan.

On Friday evening, Helen and her friends go to the disco together.

Soon they are dancing. Helen tells the others how nervous she is. She can see Tom on the other side of the room. She knows he's watching her. At last the DJ plays some slow tracks.

'Let's get a drink and sit down for a while,' suggests Helen.

The girls get some cans of cola and sit down to watch the dancing.

'I really want to get together with Tom tonight. I'm mad about him!' Helen tells the others.

'You're crazy!' smiles Jo. 'I think we're all too young to get serious.'

Sophie nods. 'I like boys as friends. Right now I don't want anything else.'

Just then, Tom walks across the room towards Helen.

'Would you like to dance?' he asks with a grin.

Helen smiles back at him and stands up. Helen and Tom dance all the slow tracks. They hold each other tightly.

At the end of

Puberty

As children grow into adults, their bodies go through a time of big change called puberty. For some children this begins at about the age of nine. For many others it starts a few years later. Girls usually start puberty a little earlier than boys.

At puberty the brain produces large amounts of chemicals called hormones, which cause changes in body shape.

Teenagers grow taller and heavier. Hair starts to grow under the arms, on the arms and legs, on the face and between the legs. There are skin changes too. The hormones cause extra oils to be produced, especially over the face, back and neck. This oiliness may produce spots. Sweating increases during puberty: if left to dry, this sweat will

begin to smell, so it's important to wash every day.

All these body changes can make you feel uncomfortable for a while, especially when you are with people of the opposite sex. Hormones can also cause mood swings – from happy to sad and back again. It may feel very confusing, but it's all part

of growing up – and, sooner or later, that happens to everyone.

All sorts

You don't need to look like a model or a pop star to be attractive to the opposite sex. Bodies come in all shapes and sizes – and every shape and size can look good.

teenage changes

7

the dance, they kiss for a long time.

male and female

'Bet you've never let a boy touch you, have you?' says Jodie nastily.

She feels happy – she's been to the cinema with Tom twice now. On Saturday they're going to a party together.

Two girls called Jodie and Tess are hanging around outside. Helen doesn't know them very well.

'There's Tom Hennessy's girlfriend!' they giggle as Helen walks past.

Helen goes red. She doesn't say anything.

'Trouble is, he thinks you're a goody-goody,' sneers Tess. 'Miss Boring, he calls you!'

Helen dashes across the schoolyard.

She can hear the two girls laughing behind her back.

A group of boys is coming towards her – she sees that one of the boys is Tom! Helen wants to run away. Her face is burning with embarrassment.

As the boys pass her, she puts her head down, but she can feel Tom looking right at her. 'Hi!' he says.

'Hello!' mumbles Helen, hurrying towards the gate. **She can't wait to get home.**

8

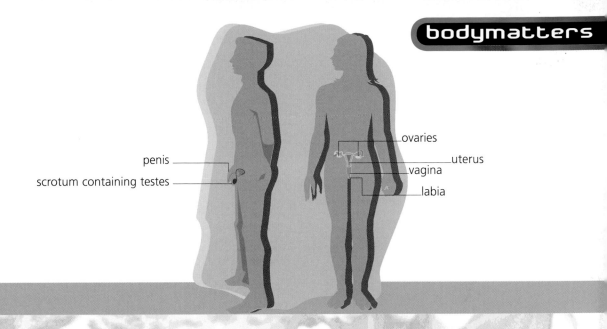

penis

scrotum containing testes

ovaries

uterus

vagina

labia

Sex organs

Like the other parts of their bodies, girls' and boys' sex organs grow during puberty. All bodies are different, so don't worry if yours doesn't look exactly like your friends'.

Girls have sex organs both outside and inside their bodies. The outside folds of skin between a girl's legs are called labia. In the centre of these is an opening called the vagina, which leads to the sex organs inside the body. Inside, a girl has a uterus (womb) where a baby can grow. Just outside the uterus, but attached to it, are two ovaries containing the eggs to make babies. A girl's breasts grow and develop at puberty to enable her to produce milk if she has a baby to feed.

Boys' sex organs are outside their bodies. A boy has two balls called testes that hang between his legs in a bag of skin called the scrotum. From puberty until old age, the testes produce millions of tiny, male sex cells called sperm. Just above the testes hangs the boy's penis, which is usually soft and limp.

9

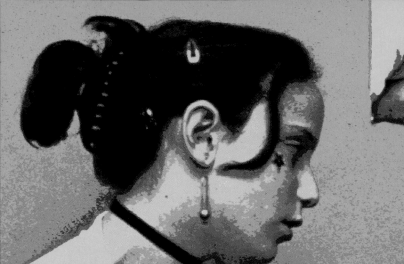

On Saturday evening, Helen, Jo and Sophie are at Jo's house getting ready for the party.

Jo's mum has offered to take them.

'What time are you meeting Tom?' asks Jo. 'Eight o'clock,' Helen tells her. She sits down on the bed. 'Do you think it's true that he calls me a goody-goody?' she asks, frowning.

'Of course not!' replies Jo.

'Ignore Tess and Jodie,' says Sophie. 'It's nothing to do with them.'

'I don't want Tom to think I'm pathetic,' says Helen quietly.

'Sophie's right. Ignore them!' says Jo fiercely, sitting down on the bed next to Helen. She's very pale.

'Are you OK?' asks Helen.

'I've just started my period,' Jo tells her. 'I've got cramp. I'll be all right in a minute.'

The girls sit waiting for Jo's mum. At last they hear her jangling her car keys.

'Ready, girls?' calls Jo's mum.

'Ready!' they all

menstruation

Jo has her period. This is also called menstruation and it begins about halfway through puberty. Girls and women usually menstruate once a month until they are about fifty years old. Girls are born with a store of eggs in their ovaries. From puberty onwards, hormones cause the ovaries to release one ripe egg every month. Each egg is about the size of a pinhead. The egg travels down the fallopian tube towards the uterus. It then passes out of the girl's vagina, along with some of the lining of the uterus and some blood. A period lasts from between two and eight days every month.

Period pain

Jo has cramp. During a period it's normal to feel a dragging pain deep below your stomach and at the top of your legs. A hot-water bottle or a warm bath may help. Before a period, some girls and women may also have mood swings and be tearful. If you feel really bad, talk to a doctor.

Towels or tampons?

There are two ways of soaking up the menstrual blood. Towels or pads fit inside your underwear. They must be changed every few hours and thrown away. Tampons are sausage-shaped and fit inside your vagina. They soak up the blood before it leaves your body. Again, they must be changed every few hours. A very rare disease called toxic-shock syndrome has been linked with tampon use. The illness feels like flu, with a sudden fever, rash and dizziness. If you develop this and are wearing a tampon, take it out and contact a doctor.

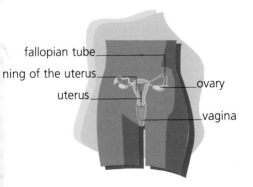

fallopian tube
ning of the uterus
uterus
ovary
vagina

shout, laughing.

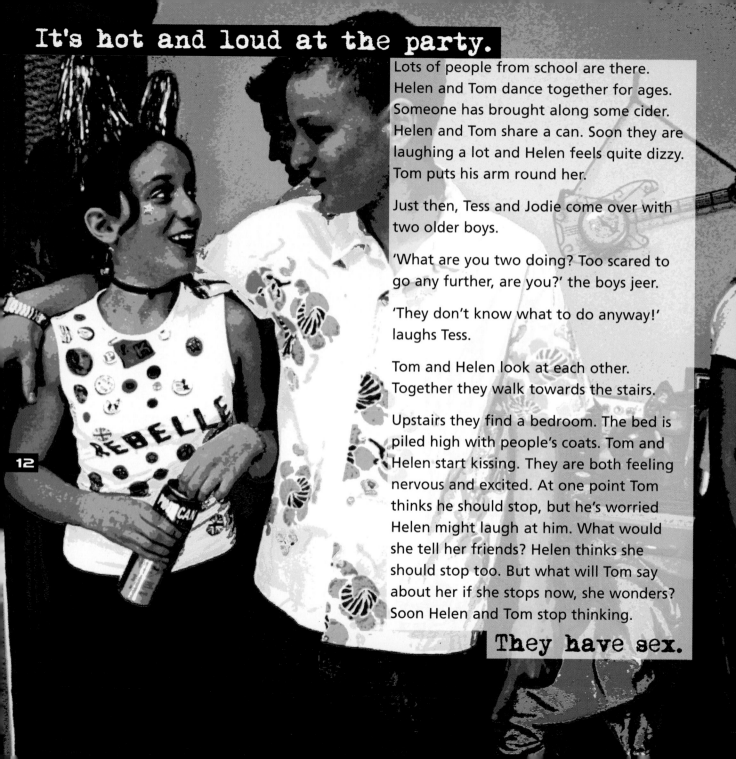

Lots of people from school are there. Helen and Tom dance together for ages. Someone has brought along some cider. Helen and Tom share a can. Soon they are laughing a lot and Helen feels quite dizzy. Tom puts his arm round her.

Just then, Tess and Jodie come over with two older boys.

'What are you two doing? Too scared to go any further, are you?' the boys jeer.

'They don't know what to do anyway!' laughs Tess.

Tom and Helen look at each other. Together they walk towards the stairs.

Upstairs they find a bedroom. The bed is piled high with people's coats. Tom and Helen start kissing. They are both feeling nervous and excited. At one point Tom thinks he should stop, but he's worried Helen might laugh at him. What would she tell her friends? Helen thinks she should stop too. But what will Tom say about her if she stops now, she wonders? Soon Helen and Tom stop thinking.

They have sex.

12

sexual intercourse

When a man gets sexually excited, blood rushes to his penis. It becomes stiff and hard. This is called an erection. When a woman is sexually excited, her vagina increases in size.

For a man and woman to 'have sex', the man pushes his penis into the woman's vagina. This is called sexual intercourse.

During sex, a liquid carrying sperm (semen) spurts from the penis into the vagina. This could result in the woman becoming pregnant.

Wet dreams
Erections happen often while a boy is growing up. They can be embarrassing, but they are natural. Often boys wake up in the morning with an erection. Sometimes a boy's penis becomes erect during a dream, and some semen spurts out. This is called a wet dream and is nothing to worry about.

A loving relationship
When young people first learn about sexual intercourse, many feel shocked or upset by the whole idea. Some think it sounds disgusting. Having sex is a very special way of sharing your private self. If sex takes place between two people in a loving relationship it can be a wonderful experience. If one or both of them feels pushed into sex before they are ready, or if they do not care about the other person, then the experience can be disappointing or distressing. It's far more rewarding to wait to have sex with a person you really care about and who cares about you. It's also important to wait until you are old enough to deal with all the deep feelings this kind of relationship involves.

13

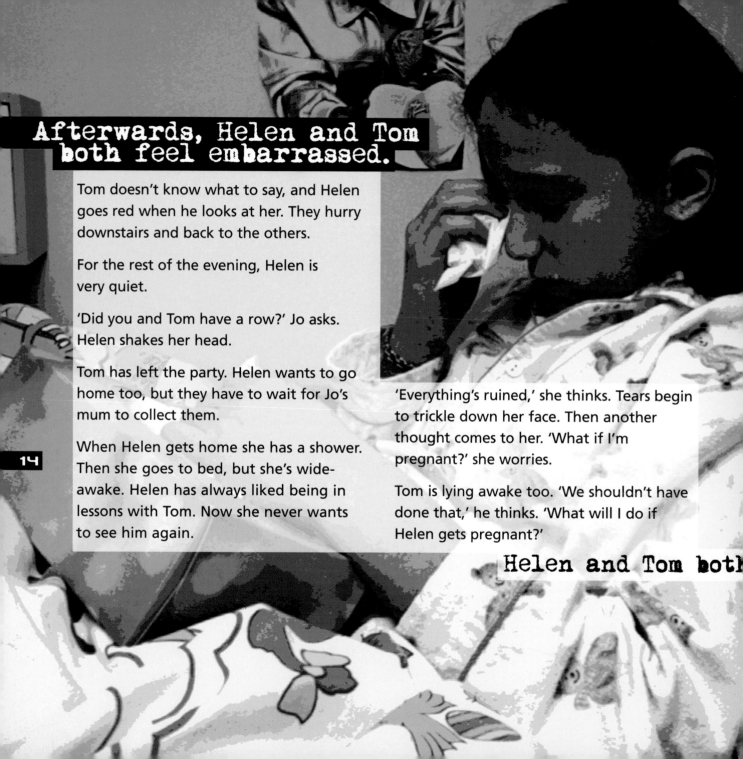

Afterwards, Helen and Tom both feel embarrassed.

Tom doesn't know what to say, and Helen goes red when he looks at her. They hurry downstairs and back to the others.

For the rest of the evening, Helen is very quiet.

'Did you and Tom have a row?' Jo asks. Helen shakes her head.

Tom has left the party. Helen wants to go home too, but they have to wait for Jo's mum to collect them.

When Helen gets home she has a shower. Then she goes to bed, but she's wide-awake. Helen has always liked being in lessons with Tom. Now she never wants to see him again.

'Everything's ruined,' she thinks. Tears begin to trickle down her face. Then another thought comes to her. 'What if I'm pregnant?' she worries.

Tom is lying awake too. 'We shouldn't have done that,' he thinks. 'What will I do if Helen gets pregnant?'

Helen and Tom bot

anxious thoughts

Fertilization

For a female to become pregnant, a male sperm needs to join up with a female egg. This is called fertilization. During sexual intercourse, some sperm travel up the

find it hard to sleep.

vagina, through the uterus and into the fallopian tubes. If a sperm meets an egg here, the egg and sperm may join together. The fertilized egg then travels to the uterus and sticks to the lining. Here the egg grows and develops and, nine months later, a baby is born.

When the sperm meet an egg they attach themselves to it. Only one sperm pierces the outside of the egg. Immediately all the other sperm let go. Below is a photo of an egg with sperm, magnified hundreds of times.

15

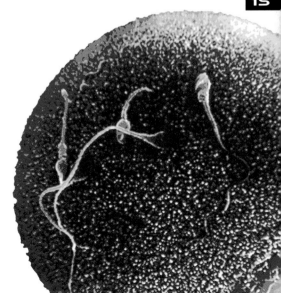

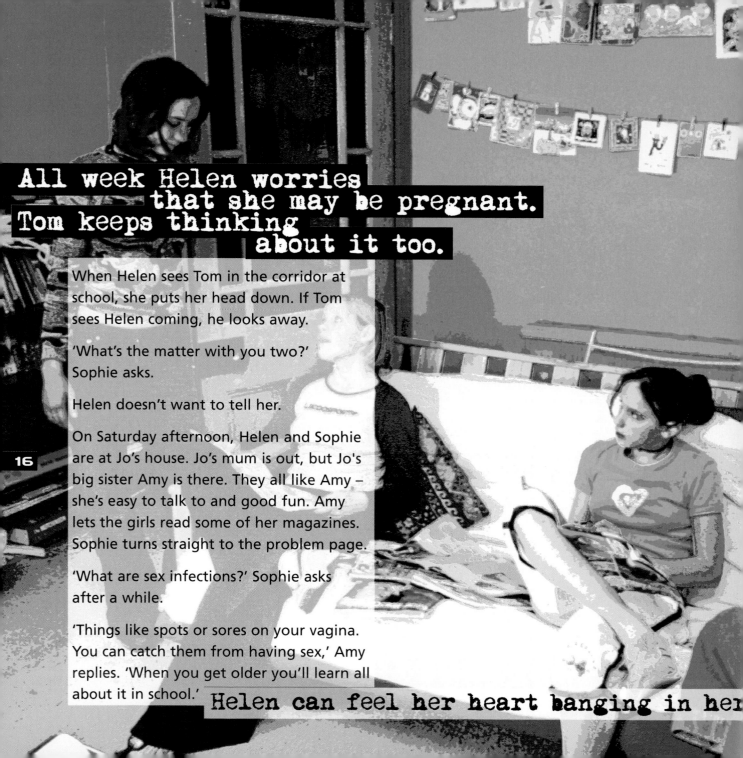

All week Helen worries that she may be pregnant. Tom keeps thinking about it too.

When Helen sees Tom in the corridor at school, she puts her head down. If Tom sees Helen coming, he looks away.

'What's the matter with you two?' Sophie asks.

Helen doesn't want to tell her.

On Saturday afternoon, Helen and Sophie are at Jo's house. Jo's mum is out, but Jo's big sister Amy is there. They all like Amy – she's easy to talk to and good fun. Amy lets the girls read some of her magazines. Sophie turns straight to the problem page.

'What are sex infections?' Sophie asks after a while.

'Things like spots or sores on your vagina. You can catch them from having sex,' Amy replies. 'When you get older you'll learn all about it in school.'

16

Helen can feel her heart banging in her

sex infections

Sex infections are mainly passed on by sexual intercourse. A girl's vagina may become itchy or sore and she may find it uncomfortable going to the toilet. There may be small blisters on her vagina or smelly dampness in her knickers. In the same way, if a boy gets an infection he may find that his penis is sore, bad-smelling, spotty or itchy. Many sex infections are very common and can be treated easily.

Most people do not carry sex infections. People who think they may have an infection should not pass it on to someone else. They should go to a doctor straight away.

They should also tell the person they have been having sex with. If left untreated, some sex infections may cause serious harm to the body.

AIDS

The most serious sexual disease is AIDS (auto-immune deficiency syndrome). It destroys the body's ability to fight off illnesses. People with AIDS die, and there is no cure. AIDS is a killer in countries all over the world. In Africa, almost fourteen million people have died from the disease. All young people everywhere need to take the threat of AIDS seriously.

Safer sex

No one wants to catch a sex infection. Some infections are not easy to spot and people may pass them on without knowing. People who are having sex can cut down their chances of getting an infection by always using a condom. This is a thin rubber tube that fits tightly over the penis. It forms a barrier between the penis and the vagina, and stops germs passing from one person to another.

17

chest. 'Maybe I've caught an infection from Tom?'
she thinks, panic-stricken.

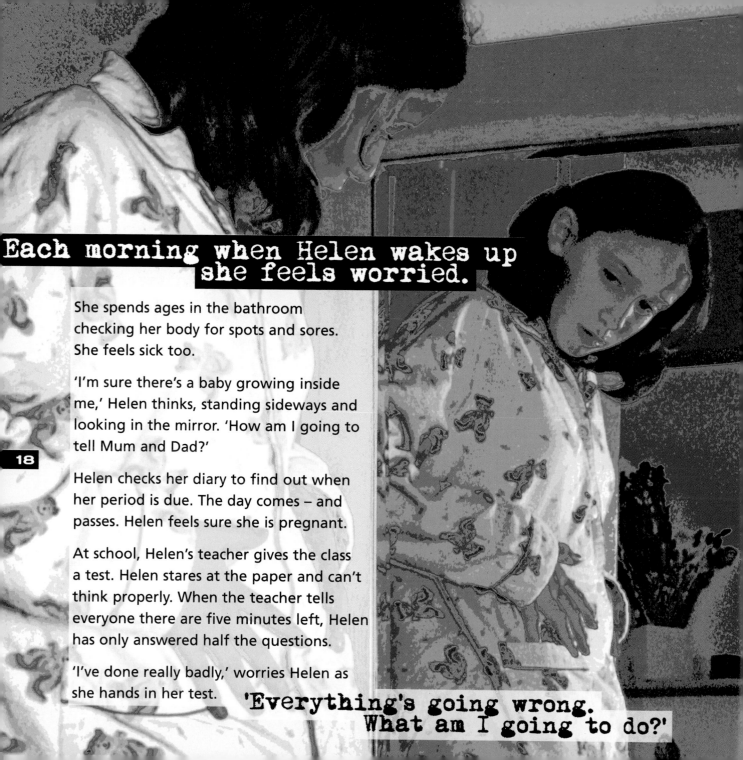

Each morning when Helen wakes up she feels worried.

She spends ages in the bathroom checking her body for spots and sores. She feels sick too.

'I'm sure there's a baby growing inside me,' Helen thinks, standing sideways and looking in the mirror. 'How am I going to tell Mum and Dad?'

Helen checks her diary to find out when her period is due. The day comes – and passes. Helen feels sure she is pregnant.

At school, Helen's teacher gives the class a test. Helen stares at the paper and can't think properly. When the teacher tells everyone there are five minutes left, Helen has only answered half the questions.

'I've done really badly,' worries Helen as she hands in her test.

'Everything's going wrong. What am I going to do?'

the first signs of pregnancy

It's a good idea for girls to keep a note of the day their last period started. Then they can count the days and know when to expect their next. Some girls have a regular period from the start. For other girls it may take several years for periods to become regular. Some girls bleed every 28 days, others every 21 days. All this is natural – but if you are worried, check it out with a doctor.

Hormones

When a woman first becomes pregnant, huge amounts of powerful female and pregnancy hormones are pumped through her body. This sudden rush of hormones can upset the stomach and the pregnant woman often feels – and is – sick.

These same hormones cause the lining of the uterus to thicken. The woman's periods stop, and do not start again until after the baby is born. In early pregnancy, the woman may feel very tired. Her breasts grow larger and may tingle. They are getting ready to produce milk for the baby. Some women may go off certain foods – and be very keen on others. All these changes are caused by the huge amounts of hormones in the pregnant woman's body.

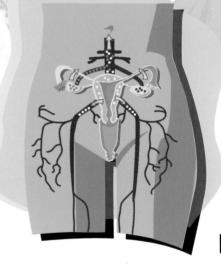

19

In early pregnancy, huge amounts of female and pregnancy hormones rush into the woman's bloodstream.

•••• oestrogen

•••• progesterone

hCG

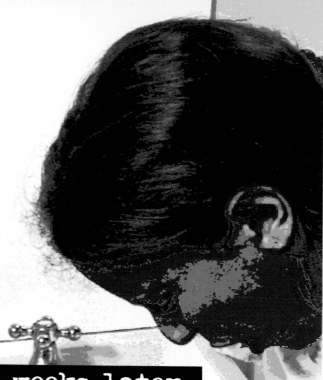

After school, Helen rushes to Jo's house looking white and tired. She sits down on Jo's bed and bursts into tears. She tells Jo and Amy the whole story.

'I don't know what to do!' she finishes, sobbing. 'I'm pregnant and my parents will go mad!'

'Calm down,' says Amy. 'Listen, first of all we'll make sure you really are pregnant, OK? You could get a pregnancy test kit from the chemist's to do at home, but I think we should go to the doctor's. She won't tell anyone. I'll phone the surgery and make an appointment with the nurse.'

Helen sits gazing into space while Amy phones the surgery. Jo comes over and gives her a hug. Soon Amy comes back smiling.

'I've made an appointment for tomorrow lunchtime,' she tells Helen. 'I'll come with you.'

'Thanks,' whispers Helen

Two weeks later, Helen wakes up feeling terrible.

She lies in bed for a little while, thinking. Her dad is cooking toast and making coffee. The smells drift into Helen's room. Suddenly she rolls out of bed, dashes to the bathroom and is sick.

'I must be pregnant,' thinks Helen. 'I'll have to tell someone.'

Helen spends all day at school worrying. She is told off three times for daydreaming.

Contraception

Helen has had unprotected sex. She may now be pregnant. If men and women want to have sex without producing children, they can use contraceptives to reduce the chances of pregnancy.

Contraception doesn't always work. The only way of making sure that pregnancy won't happen is by not having sexual intercourse. Sperm can travel, so it's also important that semen doesn't get anywhere near the vagina.

If the man and the woman don't want to have children, it's up to both of them to check that some kind of contraceptive is used before they have sex.

There are several methods of contraception. Two of these are the contraceptive pill and condoms. The pill is taken by women and girls and, if taken properly, provides very high protection against pregnancy. It stops female eggs ripening and being released. Condoms, worn by boys and men, put a barrier between the sperm and female egg. It's important that condoms are put on correctly.

finding out more

21

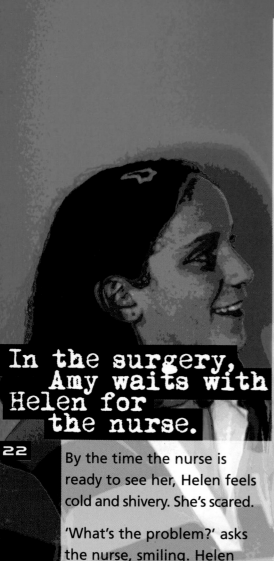

'I'm sure to be pregnant,' says Helen in a small voice. 'My period hasn't started – and I was sick yesterday morning.'

'Let's make sure,' says the nurse. 'Worry can make your period late – and it can sometimes cause you to miss a period completely. Nerves can make you sick too.'

After they've done the test, the nurse asks kindly: 'You do know that it's against the law for someone your age to have sex, don't you?'

Helen nods.

'Anyway, there are other good reasons for not having sex just now,' says the nurse. 'Your body is still very young, and regular sex at your age could give you health problems in the future. Also your mind may not be ready to cope with having a sexual relationship just yet.'

Helen nods again in agreement.

'When you're older, come back and we can talk about contraception and choose the best method for you. Your boyfriend will also need to use a condom to make sure you don't pick up an infection.'

In the surgery, Amy waits with Helen for the nurse.

By the time the nurse is ready to see her, Helen feels cold and shivery. She's scared.

'What's the problem?' asks the nurse, smiling. Helen tells her.

The nurse asks Helen's age and explains that she will do a pregnancy test.

Helen thanks the nurse

testing for pregnancy

Emergency!
If a girl or woman is not on the pill and sex takes place without a condom (or if a condom slips off or bursts), there are emergency pills. They work up to 72 hours after sex has taken place. Some doctors' surgeries, clinics and chemists keep these pills.

23

How the test works

One of the hormones produced by a pregnant woman is hCG. This hormone can be found in her urine and in her blood. A pregnancy test works by testing for hCG, either in a woman's urine or blood.

For the pregnancy test that Helen has, the nurse asks her to pass a small amount of urine into a bottle. This is sent to a laboratory for testing. Helen must wait three or four days for the results.

Pregnancy tests are carried out at doctors' surgeries, clinics and at some chemists. People can also buy test kits to do themselves at home.

and hurries back to Amy.

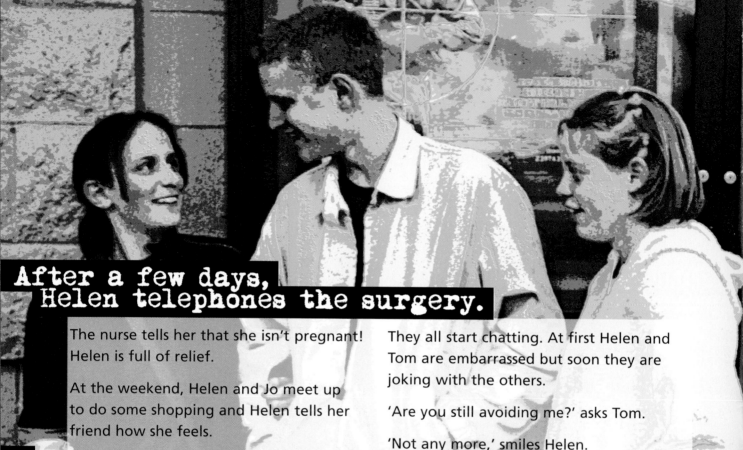

After a few days, Helen telephones the surgery.

The nurse tells her that she isn't pregnant! Helen is full of relief.

At the weekend, Helen and Jo meet up to do some shopping and Helen tells her friend how she feels.

'I'll make sure I never go through all that worry again,' she says. 'Amy was great to me. I'll buy her some bubble bath to say thank you.'

'How do you feel about Tom now?' asks Jo.

'Oh – I like him. But for now I just want to be his friend!' smiles Helen.

Later they meet Sophie to see a film. A group of boys from school is behind them in the queue. Tom's there too!

They all start chatting. At first Helen and Tom are embarrassed but soon they are joking with the others.

'Are you still avoiding me?' asks Tom.

'Not any more,' smiles Helen.

'And you're OK?' he asks quietly.

Helen nods. 'Yes, I'm feeling loads better, thanks,' she tells him.

Tom looks relieved.

'Are you two friends again?' asks Sophie.

'Yes,' say Helen and Tom at the same time.

Laughing, they all go in

Special you

There's no one else in the world exactly like you. You're special. Your body belongs to you, and you must choose whom you share it with.

To be attractive to others, you need to feel good about yourself. Most people are unhappy with some part of their body. So focus on the parts you like! Stand in front of a mirror and decide which are your best features. Make the most of what you have.

Keep yourself clean. Fresh bodies are more attractive than smelly ones! Keep your mouth clean too. Food can stick between your teeth and rot there, so floss and brush every day. To keep your breath sweet, brush your tongue too. At the end of every day, write down one good thing you've achieved. It could be something small (remembering to say thank you) or something big (tidying your room!) After two weeks you'll be able to see what a great person you are.

looking good
feeling good 25

to watch the film together.

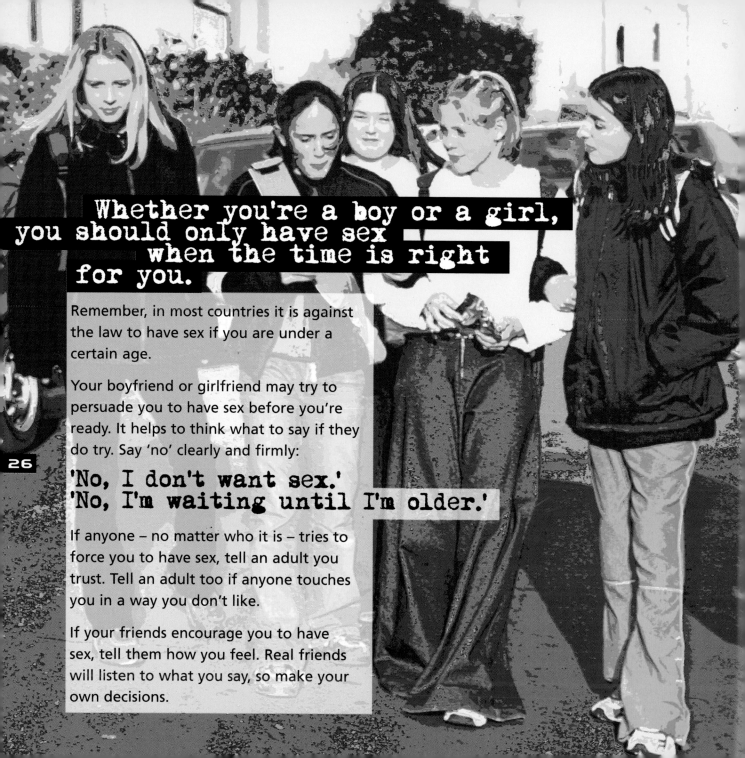

Whether you're a boy or a girl, you should only have sex when the time is right for you.

Remember, in most countries it is against the law to have sex if you are under a certain age.

Your boyfriend or girlfriend may try to persuade you to have sex before you're ready. It helps to think what to say if they do try. Say 'no' clearly and firmly:

'No, I don't want sex.'
'No, I'm waiting until I'm older.'

If anyone – no matter who it is – tries to force you to have sex, tell an adult you trust. Tell an adult too if anyone touches you in a way you don't like.

If your friends encourage you to have sex, tell them how you feel. Real friends will listen to what you say, so make your own decisions.

growing up

It's often easy to get carried away by other people's ideas. You want to fit in. You don't want to look silly. And the pressure to do what you think the others are doing can be great. But remember, your body belongs to you. The only reason for doing anything is because you want to, and you feel it is right for you.

During puberty, the following changes take place:

Girls
- breasts grow rounder and fuller from nine years of age
- hair grows around the vagina
- girls begin to grow taller and heavier
- a little yellow or white liquid may stain a girl's knickers; this is a sign that her period may start in about a year
- underarm hair begins to grow
- most girls get their first period between the ages of nine and fifteen years

Boys
- from nine years of age, the boy's testes and scrotum get bigger; then his penis grows
- hair grows around his penis, on his face and chest and under his arms
- semen may come from his penis when he has an erection
- a boy's muscles develop and he may grow as much as 40-120mm in one year
- his voice gets deeper and for a while may suddenly wobble, or 'break'

Remember:
Babies need lots of care, attention and understanding. Before you use your body to make a baby, you should be very sure that you are grown up enough in your mind.

safer sex facts

Unprotected sex is risky.

People who have unprotected sex are in danger of causing an unwanted pregnancy and catching a sex infection.

Having safer sex means:

- always using a new condom every time you have sex
- checking that the other person has no rashes, sores or spots around his penis or her vagina

When men and women are having a sexual relationship it's natural for them to touch each other's bodies. They should remember that if even a little semen escapes near the woman's vagina, it is possible for her to become pregnant.

Sex infection facts

- each year, more than one out of twenty of the world's young teenagers catches a sex infection
- there are more than twenty different sex infections
- nearly two thirds of people who have a sex infection are under 25 years of age
- if caught early, most sex infections can be treated – if someone has an infection, they should go straight to their doctor or a clinic
- sex infections can spread to the uterus and fallopian tubes – they can cause women to become infertile (unable to have a baby)

Teenage parents

Being a teenage parent means:

- less time with your friends: babies and children need constant care and attention
- less time for yourself
- less sleep for you (babies wake up often through the night)
- less money: babies and children are expensive. One pack of 48 disposable nappies costs about £6.00. A baby uses about 2,555 nappies in a year!
- less education for you: becoming a young parent could interrupt your education. When you're older, it may be difficult to find a job you enjoy without examination certificates.

Babies born to teenagers are often smaller and weaker. They are more likely to die in their first year. The very young mother is at risk too. Her bones may not have finished growing, which may make it difficult for the baby to be born.

glossary

condom a thin rubber tube that fits tightly over the penis to stop sperm or germs getting through

contraception methods used to try to reduce the chances of pregnancy

erection the state of the penis when it is stiff and hard

fallopian tube one of a pair of thin tubes through which a female egg can pass from an ovary to the uterus

fertilization the joining of a male sex cell (sperm) with a female sex cell (egg) so that a baby may be made

hormones chemicals produced in humans and other animals, which act as messengers between one part of the body and another

menstruation the monthly bleeding experienced by girls and women who are not pregnant

puberty a time of change and growth which comes at the end of childhood and the beginning of adulthood

sex cells the tiny sperm cells in a male or the egg cells in a woman which can join together to make a baby

sex organs the parts of the body which enable a man and a woman to have sex and make a baby. The sex organs of a male are the testicles and penis. The sex organs of a female are the labia, vagina, uterus and ovaries.

sexual intercourse also called 'having sex', this is when a man's stiff penis is pushed inside a woman's vagina. When a couple have loving feelings for each other, sexual intercourse is usually very pleasant for both people. It can result in pregnancy.

toxic shock syndrome a rare, dangerous illness which can be caused by using tampons

wet dream the release of semen from a boy's penis during sleep. Wet dreams are a natural part of growing up.

further information

Getting Help

If you have a problem with sex or relationships, there are people who can help. Talk to an adult you trust. Go to your doctor. You could also phone one of the offices listed below. Sometimes the telephone lines are busy. If they are, don't give up – keep trying.

Brook

Freephone 0800 0185023

Kidscape

020 7730 3300

A national charity helping children and young people to stay safe.

The Samaritans

08457 909090

ChildLine

Freephone 0800 1111

websites

http://www.brook.org.uk

http:// www.childline.org.uk

index

The numbers in **bold** refer to illustrations.